Diet recommendations for TCM - Kidney - Jing deficiency

Please check these recommendations always with a TCM nutrition consultant, therapist, doctor or dietician. The recipes and the list of ingredients are supporting also the conventional medical therapy. The calorie disclosures of fresh ingredients (fruit and vegetables) vary according to quality and time of harvest. The contents were checked by a dietician and a nutrition consultant for the Traditional Chinese Medicine (TCM).

Author:
©2017 Josef Miligui
www.ebns.at

AF236111

Source:
The lists are created from the EBNS database for nutritional counseling. The database is used by dietitians, therapists and doctors for advising the patient / client.

Literature:
The specialist literature and the training documents of the German and Austrian dietary and traditional Chinese medicine serve as a knowledge base. We have used the documents as a basis of knowledge, adapted it to our experience and completed them.
http://di-book.com

Title Photo:
©2008 Erika Weixlbaumer

Production and publishing:
BoD – Books on Demand, Norderstedt
ISBN: 9783752861426

Diet recommendations for TCM - Kidney - Jing deficiency

1   Treatment strategy

Nourish kidney essence.

2   Avoid

n.a.

3   Breakfast

	kkal. per serving
Carrot and rice gruel soup	101
Celery juice	33
Cooling rice dish with grapefruit	234

4 Snack

5 Lunch

9 Recipes

(recommendable) = You can use more.
(little) = You should use less than specified or omit.

9.1 8 treasures of rice

Strengthens kidney and bladder, builds up Qi, strengthens the spleen, repels moisture, reduces internal heat, prevents cancer, builds heart, calms nerves.
Cooking time approx. 1 hour
Calories p. portion: 212
4 portions

Quantity of ingredients
Lily bulbs 1 table spoon / 5g. (recommended)................................. *
Longane 1 table spoon / 5g. (little)... *
King Solomon's-seal 1 table spoon / 5g. (recommended)................ *
Yam root, yam root tuber 1 table spoon / 5g. (recommended).......... *
Coix (seeds) YiYi Ren 1 table spoon / 5g. (yes).............................. *
Rice wild (nature rice) 1 1/2 cups / 240g. (recommended).......... metal
Water 8-10 cups / 800g. (yes) .... earth

Cooking instructions:
Each one 1 tbsp: Bai He, Longan, Yu Zhu, Da Zao, Shan Yao, Lian Mi, Yi Yi Ren, Qian Shi
Add hot water and soak for about 30 minutes. Then add 1 - 2 cups of rice (normal) and simmer for 1/2 to 1 hour until the rice is very soft. Or: Cook for about 3 hours with the herbs a congee. Then the herbs do not have to be soaked.

9.2   Basic recipe for a beef broth (clear)

Strengthens Qi and Yang, is very warming.
Cooking time approx. 4-8 hours
Calories p. portion: 114
10 portions
Allergens: O

Quantity of ingredients

Beef soup meat 1,1 lbs / 500g. .... earth
Beef meatbones 5/8 oz / 200g. .... earth
Vinegar (Red wine vinegar) 1 dash / 3g. .... wood
Juniper berry 8 pieces / 6g. .... fire
Rosemary 1 pinch / 1g. .... fire
Carrot 3 pieces / 210g. .... earth
Parsnip 2 pieces / 300g. .... fire
Leek 1 piece / 200g. ....metal
Ginger fresh 1/2 teaspoon / 5g. ....metal
Lovage 1 stem / 15g. ....metal
Clove 2 pieces / 2g. ....metal
Pimento 6 pieces / 12g. ....metal
Anise (Common Fennel) 2 pieces / 1g. .... earth
Salt 1 teaspoon / 5g. ....water
Water 3,3 lbs / 1300g. .... earth

Cooking instructions:
Heat water, a dash of red wine vinegar, some juniper berries, a little rosemary, bones and meat till it boils; add carrot, parsnip, leek, ginger, lovage, clove, allspice, star anise and a little salt; simmer for 4-8 hours then strain.
Refrigerate for later use.

9.3   Basic recipe for a chicken broth worming

Strengthens Qi and blood, is very warm.
Cooking time approx. 2-3 hours
Calories p. portion: 90
9 portions
Allergens: L

Quantity of ingredients

Chicken meat 1/2 piece / 600g. ....wood
Carrot 2 pieces / 150g. .... earth
Leek 1 stick / 45g. ....metal
Celery root 1 piece / 500g. .... earth
Ginger fresh 2 slices / 2g. ....metal
Fenugreek (Trigonella foenum-graecum) 1 teaspoon / 2g. ....*
Juniper berry 1 teaspoon / 3g. .... fire
Bay leaf 3 pieces / 2g. ....*
Water 4 cup / 900g. .... earth

Cooking instructions:
Remove chicken parts from fat. Place chicken pieces in a saucepan with hot water and heat till it boils briefly, skimming any resulting foam. Add coarsely chopped vegetables and all spices and cook over medium heat for 2 to 3 hours. Strain the finished soup. Throw away vegetables and bones.
Tip: If you want to use the meat as a soup insert, take out after 45 minutes and return only the bones in the soup.
Refrigerate for later use.

9.4   Basic recipe for a duck broth

Forces Qi, strengthens blood and fluids, nourishes Yin, forces stomach, cools heat, strengthens spleen and liver.
Cooking time approx. 2-3 hours
Calories p. portion: 61
6 portions
Allergens: L

Quantity of ingredients

Duck (heart) 5/8 oz / 200g. .... wood
Water 2 cup / 450g. .... earth
Duck (slaughtered) 1/4 lbs - 4oz / 100g. .... wood
Carrot 2 pieces / 100g. .... earth
Celery root 1/2 piece / 600g. .... earth

Cooking instructions:
Cook duck pieces with vegetables for 2-3 hours. Sift broth through a fine sieve and refrigerate for later use.
The innards can be reused: You cut them finely and leaves them for a few minutes with fresh vegetables in the broth draw. Sprinkle with parsley before serving.

9.5 Basic recipe for a reissue soup (Congee)

Warms the stomach and spleen, harmonizes the intestine, forces Qi, reduces moisture.
Cooking time approx. 2-4 hours
Calories p. portion: 140
3 portions
Allergens:

Quantity of ingredients
Rice variety any 1 cup / 120g. ....metal
Water 6 cups / 700g. .... earth

Cooking instructions:
Cook rice and water in a ratio of about 1: 6. The amount of water determines the thickness of the mash (matter of taste).
Put the rice in a saucepan with a heavy lid. It is important to simmer the rice after a short boil on the slightest flame, otherwise it burns.
Boil the rice for 2-4 hours. The longer he cooks, the more he strengthens.
If you want to eat the dish for breakfast, you can put the rice on just before bedtime.
To be on the safe side, you should first check the behavior of your pot and cooker under observation for a similar amount of time, so that nothing burns.
Refrigerate for later use.

9.6 Basic recipe for a vegetable soup, nutritious

Strengthens spleen and lung, regulates Qi flow, builds up Qi, dries out, passes downwardly, strengthens stomach Qi.
Cooking time approx. 2-3 hours
Calories p. portion: 48
5 portions
Allergens: L

Quantity of ingredients
Olive oil 1 table spoon / 4g. .... earth
Onion white 1 piece / 60g. ....metal
Carrot 3 pieces / 200g. .... earth
Parsnip 3/8 lbs - 6oz / 150g. .... fire
Celery root 1 cup / 100g. .... earth
Ginger fresh 1/2 teaspoon / 2g. ....metal

Lemon 1/2 piece / 25g. ....wood
Juniper berry 6 pieces / 6g. .... fire
Thyme dried 1 pinch / 1g. ....metal
Lovage 1 table spoon / 3g. ....metal
Bay leaf 2 leaves / 1g. ....*
Salt 1 pinch / 1g. ....water
Water 3 cups / 650g. .... earth

Cooking instructions:
Cut the vegetables into cubes.
Heat oil in hot pot, fry shortly onions and vegetables.
Add cold water, then add ginger, bay leaf and lemon juice.
Season with juniper, thyme and lovage. Cover for 2 - 3 hours on a low heat and simmer.
The used vegetables should be thrown away.
The basic recipe serves as a soup base and to refine vegetables, legumes or cereals.
If you want to eat vegetable soup immediately, add the desired vegetables half an hour before.
Refrigerate for later use.

9.7   Carrot and rice gruel soup

Warms the stomach and spleen, harmonizes the intestine, forces Qi, reduces moisture, strengthens spleen and liver, regulates Qi flow, moisturizes, relaxes, builds up Qi, spreads.
Cooking time approx. 10 min
Calories p. portion: 101
1 portions

Quantity of ingredients
Basic recipe for a rice soup (Congee) 1 cup / 120g. (recommended) *
Carrot 2 pieces / 100g. (yes) .... earth
Salt 1 teaspoon / 4g. (recommended)......................................water

Cooking instructions:
Peel and grate carrots. Heat the rice soup (according to the basic recipe) till it boils and add the grated carrots and salt. Cook for 10 minutes.

9.8 Celery juice

Strengthens stomach Qi, moisturizes, relaxes, builds up Qi, spreads.
Cooking time approx. 5 min
Calories p. portion: 33
1 portions
Allergens: L

Quantity of ingredients
Celery root 1/2 piece / 200g. (recommended)............................ earth
Water 1 cup / 120g. (yes)... earth
Salt 1 pinch / 0,5g. (recommended)...water

Cooking instructions:
Peel celeriac and cut into pieces and juice. Mix with water and salt as
needed.

9.9 Chicken soup with angelica root and buckthorn fruit

Strengthens spleen and nourishes the blood and Yin of the liver, forces
Qi and blood, is very warming.
Cooking time approx. 1 1/2 hours
Calories p. portion: 77
3 portions
Allergens: LO

Quantity of ingredients
Basic recipe for a chicken soup 2 cup / 500g. (recommended) ....*
Angelica root 1/8 oz / 5g. (recommended) ....*
Bocksdorn fruits, goji berry dried 1/8 lbs - 2oz / 50g. ....wood

Cooking instructions:
When you cook chicken broth according to basic recipes add angelica
root and Bocksdorn fruits in the last 40 minutes.

Ingestion: Drink 2-3 cups of broth daily.

9.10 Cooling rice dish with grapefruit

Lowers lung Qi, nourishes fluids, dissolves mucus, dries out, passes downwardly, warms the stomach and spleen, harmonizes the intestine, forces Qi, reduces moisture, strengthens Qi and Kidney Jing, moisturizes, relaxes, builds up Qi, spreads.
Cooking time approx. 20 min
Calories p. portion: 234
4 portions
Allergens: GHO

Quantity of ingredients
Rice round grain 1 cup / 120g. (recommended) .... metal
Water 5 cups / 600g. (yes) .... earth
Hazelnuts 2 table spoons / 20g. (yes) .... earth
Raisins 2 table spoons / 20g. (little) .... earth
Agave nectar 1 table spoon / 10g. (recommended) .... *
Salt 1 pinch / 0,2g. (recommended) .... water
Almond puree 1 table spoon / 10g. (little) .... earth
Grapefruit (Pomelo) 1 piece / 200g. (little) .... fire
Butter organic 2 teaspoons / 20g. (yes) .... earth

Cooking instructions:
Preparation on the eve: Pour round grain rice into cold water and cook. Soak chopped hazelnuts and raisins in some hot water overnight.

In the morning: Stir in a little hot water some agave syrup; add the rice and heat; add a small pinch of salt, almond paste, chopped grapefruit, the soaked chopped hazelnuts and raisins and mix; Serve with a small piece of butter.

9.11 Cucumber soup

Cools and moisturizes, diuretic, reduces damp heat, detoxifies, relaxes, builds up Qi, spreads, distributes mucus, passes downwardly, activates Wei Qi, forces Qi.
Cooking time approx. 20 min
Calories p. portion: 96
4 portions
Allergens: M

Quantity of ingredients

Olive oil 2 table spoons / 35g. (recommended) .... earth
Cucumber 2 pieces / 400g. (recommended) .... earth
Water 2 cup / 500g. (yes) .... earth
Sage 3 leaves / 3g. (yes).. fire
Mustard 1/2 teaspoon / 0,5g. (recommended) ....metal
Coriander 1 pinch / 1g. (yes) ....metal
Cardamom 1 pinch / 1g. (recommended)... *
Salt 1 pinch / 1g. (recommended)..water

Cooking instructions:
Heat oil and roast short the small cucumbers. Add Mustard seeds,
coriander, cardamom and salt. Add water. Simmer for 10-15 min. Puree
and decorate with fresh chopped sage.

9.12 Grape compote

Moisturizes, relaxes, builds up Qi, spreads, moisten the lungs and large
intestine.
Cooking time approx. 10 min
Calories p. portion: 128
1 portions
Allergens: H

Quantity of ingredients

Grapes red 3/8 lbs - 6oz / 150g. (recommended)....................... earth
Water 4 table spoons / 30g. (yes)... earth
Almond 1 teaspoon / 3g. (yes).. earth

Cooking instructions:
Remove the grapes from the stems, wash thoroughly in warm water
and drain. Halve the grapes (remove the seeds for babies). In a small
saucepan, heat 4 tablespoons of water with the grapes and the grated
almonds till it boils . Cook over low heat for about 3 minutes, then chill.
(For babies lukewarm).

9.13 Grape juice (fresh, homemade)

Moisturizes, relaxes, builds up Qi, spreads.
Cooking time approx. 15 min
Calories p. portion: 73
2 portions

Quantity of ingredients
Grapes white 7/8 lbs / 200g. (recommended) .... earth

Cooking instructions:
For about 200 ml of juice, pluck 400 g of white grapes (alternatively berries or stone fruit) from the stalk, wash thoroughly, drain and halve. Fill in the sieve insert of the pressure cooker. On the bottom of the pot pour about 2 cm high water, stack the cross, the juice bowl (accessories) and the sieve with the grapes on top of each other. Close the pot and juice the grapes for about 12 minutes.

9.14 Kohlrabi Potatoes mash

Moves Qi and blood, reduces moisture, forces Qi, forces spleen, relieves inflammation, moisturizes, relaxes, builds up Qi, spreads, forces kidney Jing.
Cooking time approx. 25 min
Calories p. portion: 278
1 portions
Allergens: CG

Quantity of ingredients
Kohlrabi 1/2 piece / 150g. (yes) .... earth
Potato 1/4 lbs - 4oz / 100g. (yes) .... earth
Butter organic 1 table spoon / 10g. (yes) .... earth
Chicken yolk 1 piece / 25g. (recommended) .... earth

Cooking instructions:
Remove the kohlrabi leaves, wash the tuber and tender leaves and the potatoes thoroughly. Peel the kohlrabi and potatoes, cut into cubes about 1 cm in size. Melt half the butter in a small saucepan, add the kohlrabi and the potatoes and fry in it. Steam with 2 tablespoons of water in a closed saucepan over low heat for about 15 minutes. Meanwhile, free the tender kohlrabi leaves from the stems and chop very finely. In total, at most 2 tablespoons of leaf pieces should be used. Add this to the vegetables about 5 minutes before the end of the cooking time. Stir in the egg yolk and bring to the boil again. Put the vegetables in a plate and mix with the remaining butter and egg yolk. (Crush for the baby with a fork.)

9.15 Lentils and rice stew

Strengthens spleen and liver, regulates Qi flow, moisturizes, relaxes, builds up Qi, spreads, warms the stomach and spleen, harmonizes the intestine, forces Qi, reduces moisture, brings the liver Qi in motion, cools heat.
Cooking time approx. 25 min
Calories p. portion: 232
3 portions
Allergens: LNO

Quantity of ingredients
Lentils 1/4 lbs - 4oz / 100g. (yes)...water
Water 5 cups / 500g. (yes) .... earth
Rice variety any 1 cup / 120g. (yes)..metal
Sesame oil 1 table spoon / 10g. (yes)..................................... earth
Carrot 2 pieces / 150g. (yes) .... earth
Celery sticks 2 rods / 20g. (recommended).............................. earth
Cumin (Caraway seed) 1 pinch / 0,2g. (little) ....metal
Salt 1 pinch / 0,5g. (recommended)...water
Vinegar (Apple vinegar) 1 dash / 2g. (little) ....wood
Parsley 2 table spoons / 18g. (recommended)...........................wood

Cooking instructions:
Soak the dry lentils the day before.
Heat sesame oil in a hot pot; cut carrot and celery into small pieces and sauté; add rice, a pinch of cumin and lentils and heat till it boils.
If the lenses are soft, add salt; season with a little vinegar and garnish with parsley.

Variant: In summer you can omit the cumin and add fresh green peas, Chinese cabbage or celery.

9.16 Pear compote

Moisturizes lungs, reduces lung mucus, nourishes lungs Qi.
Cooking time approx. 20 min
Calories p. portion: 100
3 portions

Quantity of ingredients
Water 1 1/2 cups / 240g. (yes).. earth
Pear 4 / 500g. (recommended).. earth

Cooking instructions:
Halve organic pears. Cores and skin can be used. Pear in the pot and add water. Simmer for up to 20 minutes until pears are tender.

9.17 Pear juice

Moisturizes lungs, reduces lung mucus, nourishes lungs Qi.
Cooking time approx. 5 min
Calories p. portion: 180
2 portions

Quantity of ingredients
Pear 3 pieces / 600g. (recommended)....................................... earth

Cooking instructions:
Peel pears thinly (vitamins under the skin) and core. Juice in the juicer.

9.18 Red grape juice with egg yolk

Tonifies Yin and Qi, brings blood into motion, exudes moisture, detoxifying, hematinic.
Cooking time approx. 5 min
Calories p. portion: 271
1 portions
Allergens: C

Quantity of ingredients
Grape juice red 1 cup / 250g. (recommended)........................... earth
Chicken yolk 1 piece / 25g. (recommended) .... earth

Cooking instructions:
Whisk egg yolks in grape juice.

9.19 Rice congee with carrots and fennel

Nutritious builds up Qi, forces the digestive functions.
Cooking time approx. 2 hours and more
Calories p. portion: 131
3 portions
Allergens: G

Quantity of ingredients
Basic recipe for a rice soup 2 cup / 500g. (recommended)................*
Carrot 2 pieces / 100g. (yes) .... earth

Fennel 1 piece / 250g. (recommended) .... earth
Butter organic 1 teaspoon / 3g. (yes)... earth
Cardamom 1/2 teaspoon / 1g. (recommended)................................*

Cooking instructions:
Cook rice congee according to basic recipe.
Clean and cut carrots and fennel.

When carrots and fennel are cooked from the beginning, they serve
wholesomeness. If added shortly before the end of the cooking time,
taste and vitamins are retained.

Refine with butter and cardamom before serving.

9.20 Rice congee with honey pear and black sesame

Especially good in kidney Yin deficiency, moisturizes lungs, cools heat,
reduces lung mucus, produces humors, moisturizes, relaxes, builds up
Qi, spreads, moisturizes intestines, nourishes Yin.
Cooking time approx. 10 min - 3 hours
Calories p. portion: 158
2 portions
Allergens: N

Quantity of ingredients
Basic recipe for a rice soup 1 1/2 cups / 240g. (recommended) ....*
Pear 2 pieces / 300g. (recommended)...................................... earth
Sesame, black 1 teaspoon / 3g. (recommended)....................... wood

Cooking instructions:
Cook rice congee according to basic recipe.
Fill pot with 3 cm of water and heat till it boils. Quarter the pears (with
the skin and seeds) and simmer them covered with black sesame for 10
minutes. Mix with the rice.

9.21 Rice congee with mung beans

Warms the stomach and spleen, harmonizes the intestine, forces Qi,
reduces moisture, reduces heat, softens, passes downwardly,
moisturizes, laxative, antiparasitic.
Cooking time approx. 2 hours
Calories p. portion: 424
2 portions

Quantity of ingredients
Basic recipe for a rice soup 4 cups / 500g. (recommended)..............*
Mung bean 1/2 cup / 50g. (recommended) ....water
Herbs various 2 table spoons / 8g. (recommended).........................*
Rapeseed oil 2 table spoons / 20g. (yes)................................. earth

Cooking instructions:
Soak the mung beans the day before and strain. Cook the rice according to the basic recipe and cook the mung beans with the rice.

Finally, add fresh herbs and a dash of high-quality cold-pressed oil.

9.22 Rice porridge with shrubs (seeds) Yi Yi Ren

Warms stomach, harmonizes the intestine, forces Qi, reduces moisture, forces spleen, nourishes and forces Lunge, reduces internal heat, moves Qi and blood, diuretic, cools in internal heat.
Cooking time approx. 25 min
Calories p. portion: 212
2 portions

Quantity of ingredients
Water 4 cups / 450g. (yes) .... earth
Rice variety any 1 cup / 120g. (yes)...metal
Lemon peel 1/4 piece / 2g. (recommended)................................. fire
Coix (seeds) YiYi Ren 1/2 cup / 50g. (yes) ....*
Cress 1 table spoon / 6g. (recommended)................................metal

Cooking instructions:
Cook rice porridge according to basic recipe with a half cup of Yi Yi Ren and lemon peel. Simmer for 1 hour and then sprinkle cress over it.

9.23 Rice with berries

Preserves the fluids, contracts, forces kidney and bladder, moisturizes intestines, nourishes blood and Yi, cools heat, distributes mucus, derives wind-cold and wind-heat, brings the stomach Qi in motion, solves congestion.
Cooking time approx. 5 min
Calories p. portion: 160
4 portions
Allergens: N

Quantity of ingredients

Rice wild (nature rice) 1 cup / 120g. (recommended) .... metal
Water 6 cups / 700g. (yes) .... earth
Sunflower seeds 2 table spoons / 20g. (recommended) .... earth
Sesame, white 2 table spoons / 18g. (yes) .... earth
Berries of the season 1 cup / 120g. (recommended) .... wood
Vanilla 1 pinch / 0,2g. (yes) .... *
Peppermint 2 leaves (chopped) / 2g. (recommended) .... metal
Anise (Common Fennel) 1 pinch / 1g. (little) .... earth

Cooking instructions:
Warm 2 ladles of boiled rice congee according to basic recipe. Add sunflower seeds or sesame seeds. Serve in a bowl, sprinkle with fresh berries. Sweetening as needed.

Spices: vanilla, fresh mint, anise

Summer: plum (tastes good with grated nutmeg)
Winter: pickled cherries, grated apple, jam with a lot of fruit content.

9.24 Rice with parsnips

Regulates Qi, dries out, passes downwardly, warms the stomach and spleen, harmonizes the intestine, forces Qi, reduces moisture. moisturizes, relaxes, builds up Qi, spreads. distributes mucus, activates Wei Qi, forces Qi.
Cooking time approx. 45 min
Calories p. portion: 206
3 portions

Quantity of ingredients

Rice variety any 1 cup / 120g. (yes) .... metal
Water 1 1/2 cups / 200g. (yes) .... earth
Salt 1 pinch / 1g. (recommended) .... water
Parsnip 3-4 pieces / 450g. (recommended) .... fire
Olive oil 1 table spoon / 10g. (recommended) .... earth
Sage 1 teaspoon / 3g. (yes) .... fire

Cooking instructions:
Peel the parsnips and cut into slices. Fry for a short time in oil. Add the rice and fry again for a short time. Add the water and cook it at least 30 min. Sprinkle with fresh chopped sage.

9.25 Rice with stewed vegetables

Dissipates heat and moisture.
Cooking time approx. 20 min
Calories p. portion: 166
2 portions
Allergens: L

Quantity of ingredients
Rice variety any 1/2 cup / 60g. (yes)..metal
Water 3 cups / 300g. (yes) .... earth
Lemon peel 1 piece / 3g. (recommended)..................................... fire
Water 1/2 cup / 0g. (yes)... earth
Carrot 2 pieces / 180g. (yes) .... earth
Celery sticks 1/2 piece / 5g. (recommended) .... earth
Champignon 1/2 cup / 50g. (recommended)............................. earth
Cress 2 table spoons / 20g. (recommended) ....metal
Linseed oil 1 dash / 3g. (recommended)..................................... earth

Cooking instructions:
Cook rice according to basic recipe with a piece of lemon peel.
Steam chopped carrots, celery and mushrooms until soft.
Then sprinkle with cress. Then add a dash of high quality cold oil.

9.26 Roasted millet with Celery sticks

Strengthens spleen and kidney, diuretic, brings the liver Qi in motion,
cools heat, moisturizes, relaxes, builds up Qi, spreads.
Cooking time approx. 30 min
Calories p. portion: 400
2 portions
Allergens: L

Quantity of ingredients
Millet 1 cup / 120g. (yes) .... earth
Water 1 1/2 cups / 240g. (yes)...................................... earth
Celery sticks 2 rods / 50g. (recommended)............................. earth
Water 2 table spoons / 30g. (yes)................................... earth
Herbs various 1 table spoon / 10g. (recommended).........................*
Salt 1 pinch / 1g. (recommended)...water
Sage 3-4 leaves / 2g. (yes)... fire
Cress 1 teaspoon / 3g. (recommended)..................................metal

Cooking instructions:
Roast millet briefly, pour over water, heat till it boils and let stand for 20 min. to swell.

Cut celery into small pieces and mix with water, salt and fresh herbs and cook for 10 min. Add to the millet. Sprinkle fresh sage or watercress over it.

9.27 Roasted nuts

Strengthens kidney Qi, essence and brain, forces kidney, builds up essence, warms lungs, moistens the intestine, moisturizes, relaxes, builds up Qi, spreads.
Cooking time approx. 5 min
Calories p. portion: 973
2 portions
Allergens: H

Quantity of ingredients
Hazelnuts 1/4 lbs - 4oz / 100g. (yes)..................................... earth
Cashews 1/4 lbs - 4oz / 100g. (yes).. earth
Walnuts 1/4 lbs - 4oz / 100g. (recommended)........................... earth

Cooking instructions:
Roast nuts in a pan for about 5 minutes.

9.28 Soup with cucumbers and tomatoes

Reduces damp heat, nourishes liver-Yin, cools heat, produces humors, calms nerves and stomach.
Cooking time approx. 10 min
Calories p. portion: 137
2 portions
Allergens: CO

Quantity of ingredients
Cucumber 1 piece / 300g. (recommended)................................ earth
Tomato 4 pieces (very ripe) / 200g. (recommended)..................wood
Onion white 1 piece / 50g. (little)...metal
Peppers 1/2 piece (green) / 10g. (recommended)...................... earth
Salt 1 pinch / 0,5g. (recommended)...water
Vinegar (Apple vinegar) 1 dash / 2g. (little) ....wood
Water 1 cup / 120g. (yes) .... earth
Chicken egg 2 pieces / 120g. (recommended)........................... earth

Cooking instructions:
Puree all ingredients in the blender. Cool in the fridge. When serving, sprinkle with chopped breadcrumbs and finely chopped boiled egg.

9.29 Spinach with Tahini

Nourishes blood and Yin, forces Zang-organs, forces stomach and intestines, harmonizes Qi, moisturizes lungs, forces Qi, forces spleen, relieves inflammation, moisturizes, relaxes, builds up Qi, spreads, nourishes blood.
Cooking time approx. 20 min
Calories p. portion: 150
4 portions
Allergens: N

Quantity of ingredients
Potato 1,1 lbs / 500g. (yes).. earth
Salt 1 pinch / 0,2g. (recommended)...water
Water 1 cup / 25g. (yes).. earth
Spinach 2,2 lbs / 800g. (recommended) .... earth
Sesame paste (Tahini) 2 table spoons / 20g. (recommended) ... earth

Cooking instructions:
Cook potatoes and peel. Heat water. Blanch spinach. Shake off water and let it dry and stir with sesame.

9.30 Spinach flan with milk

Forces Qi, forces spleen, relieves inflammation, moisturizes, relaxes, builds up Qi, spreads, forces blood, Yin and Jing, nourishes Yin, Moisturizes in case of internal dryness, nourishes blood and Yi, forces Zang-organs.
Cooking time approx. 1 min
Calories p. portion: 250
1 portions
Allergens: ACG

Quantity of ingredients
Potato 1/4 lbs - 4oz / 100g. (yes).. earth
Spinach 1/8 lbs - 2oz / 50g. (recommended)............................. earth
Chicken egg 1 piece / 65g. (recommended)............................. earth
Breadcrumbs (wheat bread) 1 teaspoon / 3g. (recommended)... wood
Cow's milk (whole milk 3.5% fat) 6 table spoons / 50g. (little)...........*

Créme fraiche cheese 1 teaspoon / 3g. (yes)..................................*
Butter organic 1 teaspoon / 3g. (yes).. earth

Cooking instructions:
Wash the potatoes and cook with a little water in about 20 minutes.
Heat the water till it boils. Clean the fresh spinach and add to the boiling water (the frozen unfreeze), bring to the boil again and boil for about 2 minutes. Drain the spinach and puree.
Peel the potatoes and squeeze them through the potato press or crush them with the potato masher.
Mix with the spinach, egg and breadcrumbs.
Grease a small, refractory form (about 300 ml) with the butter and pour in the vegetable musk. Put the dish in a saucepan and pour enough water into the saucepan that the dish is two-thirds in a water bath.
Cover and simmer for 15 minutes over medium heat.

Heat the milk with the creme fraiche.

Put the spinach flan on a plate and pour the milk over it.

9.31 Strawberry soup with melons

Forces blood, cools blood, preserves the fluids, contracts, moisturizes, spreads, forces heart Yin.
Cooking time approx. 5 min
Calories p. portion: 87
2 portions

Quantity of ingredients
Strawberries 3/4 lbs / 300g. (recommended) .... wood
Strawberry Juice 1/3 cup / 70g. (recommended)....................... wood
Lemon peel 1/4 teaspoon / 1g. (recommended)........................... fire
Cantaloupe 5/8 oz / 200g. (recommended)............................... earth

Cooking instructions:
Puree strawberries (fresh or frozen) and strawberry juice with the blender, mix in a little sugar.
Cut melon pulp into small pieces.
Arrange strawberry soup in portions. Put the melon cubes in the sweet soup.

9.32 Tea from basil

Dries out, passes downwardly.
Cooking time approx. 10 min
Calories p. portion: 0
4 portions

Quantity of ingredients
Basil 1 teaspoon / 2g. (recommended) ....metal
Water 2 cup / 500g. (yes) .... earth

Cooking instructions:
Heat the water till it boils and put it aside. Add basil and 10 min. to let
go. Sweet to taste with honey.

9.33 Tea from celery sticks

Brings the Liver Qi in motion, cools heat, moisturizes, relaxes, builds up
Qi, spreads.
Cooking time approx. 15 min
Calories p. portion: 1
4 portions
Allergens: L

Quantity of ingredients
Celery sticks 2 table spoons (chopped) / 18g. (recommended) .. earth
Water 2 cup / 500g. (yes) .... earth

Cooking instructions:
Heat the water till it boils and put it aside. Add cutted celery and cook
for 10 min. to let go. Strain. Sweet to taste with honey.

9.34 Wheat fresh grain porridge with pears.

Moisturizes lungs, cools heat, reduces lung mucus, nourishes Yin from
heart and kidney, forces heart and kidney, moisturizes, relaxes, builds
up Qi, spreads.
Cooking time approx. 25 min
Calories p. portion: 309
2 portions
Allergens: ANO

Quantity of ingredients

Wheat 1 cup / 100g. (recommended)..wood
Water 2-4 cups / 350g. (yes) ....earth
Pear 2 pieces / 300g. (recommended)......................................earth
Raisins 1 table spoon / 10g. (little)..earth
Sesame, white 1 table spoon / 8g. (yes)...................................earth
Sunflower seeds 1 table spoon / 8g. (recommended) ....earth
Cardamom 1 pinch / 0,3g. (recommended)..*
Salt 1 pinch / 0,3g. (recommended)...water

Cooking instructions:

Preparation the night before: Wheat roughly cut; soak overnight.

In the morning: Put the wheat meal with a little hot water; simmer with stirring for about 15 minutes.
Meanwhile, add pear compote, raisins, crushed sesame, sunflower seeds, some ground cardamom, a small pinch of salt.

Variants: with grated apple or seasonal fruit.

10 Effects of food

10.1 Use ingredients: recommendable

Acai powder
Acerola fruit nectar or powder
Agar agar (kelp)
Agave nectar
Agrimony
Aloe juice
Amaranth Pops
Angelica root
Apple juice (natural cloudy)
Apple puree
Apricot dried
Apricot jam
Apricot nectar
Apricots juice
Artichoke
Asparagus (green or white)
Avocado
Baking powder
Banchatee (green tea)
barberry
Barley flour
Barley grass powder
Barley grouts
Barley malt
Basic recipe for a beef soup
Basic recipe for a beef soup (warming)
Basic recipe for a chicken soup
(warming)
Basic recipe for a duck soup
Basic recipe for a fish soup
Basic recipe for a rice soup (Congee)
Basic recipe for a vegetable soup
(nutritious)
Basil
Basil (fresh)
Bay leaf
Beans (green, fresh)
Bearberry leaf
Beef heart (calf)
Beef kidney
Beef Oxtail pieces
Beef soup meat
Beer (alcohol-free)
Beer (alcohol-reduced)
Berries of the season
Berry juice
Bitter Herb liqueur
Bitter Lemon
Bitter liqueur

Bitter orange peel
Black fungus mushroom
Blackberry dried (unripe fruit)
Blackberry jam
Blackberry leaves
Blackberry´s
Blackthorn (Sloe)
Blue mallow tee
Blueberry
Blueberry dried
Blueberry jam
Bocksdorn fruits (Fructus Lycii, Goji,
goji berry dried
Boletus mushroom
Borage
Borage oil
Brazil nuts
Bread roll
Bread with carob kernel flour
Breadcrumbs (wheat bread, bread roll)
Brie cheese
Brown ale
Brussels sprouts
Buckbean
Buckwheat (roasted) Kasha
Buckwheat whole grain
Butter (half fat)
Camembert
Campari
Cantaloupe
Capers in olive oil
Cardamom
Carob flour, St. john's bread
Carp
Caviar
Celery root
Celery sticks
Chamomile tea
Champignon
Channa-Dal
Chanterelle
Chard
Chenpi (chinese tangerine bowl)
Cherry
Cherry (sour)
Cherry compote
Chervil
Chervil dried
Chestnut puree

Chicken Blood
Chicken egg
Chicken egg white
Chicken heart
Chicken liver
Chicken meat
Chicken stomach
Chicken yolk
Chickweed
Chicory
Chinese pearl barley
Chlorella (fresh water)
Chocolate
Chocolate (Diabetic)
Chrysanthemum blossom tea
Clarified butter
Clementine
Coconut fat
Coconut meat
Codfish
Cola drink
Cola drink (low calorie)
Compote (fruits of the season)
Coriander (fresh)
Corn (fast polenta)
Corn (roasted)
Corn flour
Corn germ oil
Corn Grease (Polenta)
Corn silk tea
Corn starch
Cottage cheese
Cranberries
Cranberry
Cranberry jam
Cream (30% fat)
Cream 10% coffee cream
Cream sour 10%
Cream sour 20%
Cream sour 30%
Creamer
Cress
Crispbread
Crucian
Cucumber
Cucumber (bitter)
Cucumber (spicy cucumber)
Currant jam (black)
Currant jam (red)
Currant juice (black)
Currants (black)
Currants (red)
Daisy
Dandelion juice

Dashi
Dates red
Deer's Bones
Deer's kidneys
Duck (heart)
Duck (slaughtered)
Ducks egg
Dulse (seaweed)
Dyer's broom herb
Edam cheese
Eel smoked
Elderberries
Emmental cheese
Endive salad
Fennel
Fennel seeds ground
Fenugreek (Trigonella foenum-graecum)
Fernet Branca (herbal bitter liqueur)
Feta cheese
Fish innards
Fish pieces mixed (fresh water)
Fish remains
Fish sauce
Flounder
Flower pollen
Fox nut, gorgon nut, makhana
French beans
Fresh cheese from soya
Fresh cheese with herbs
Freshwater crab
Freshwater fish
Fructose (glucose)
Fruit mix juice
Fruit tea
Gail plum
Galangal
Garam Masala powder
Gelatin white
Gelee Royal
Gentian root
Gentian root tea
Ginkgo fruit
Ginseng
Ginseng liqueur
Ginseng root
Goat and sheep's blood
Goat and sheep's brain
Goat and sheep's liver
Goat and sheep's stomach
Goose blood
Goose fat
Gorgonzola
Gouda cheese

Grape juice red
Grape juice white
Grapefruit dried peel
Grapes red
Grapes white
Grapeseed oil
Grass carp
Greengage
Guava
Halibut (Flatfish)
Herbal tea mix
Herbs bitter
Herbs of Provence
Herbs various
Herbs wild
Herring
Hibiscus
Hibiscus tea
Hijiki
Hokkaido pumpkin
Honey wine (Met)
Hop
Horehound leaves
Horse meat
Jasmine blossoms tee
Jellyfish
Kaki plum
Kalmus
King Solomon's-seal
Kombu seaweed (Saccharina japonica)
Kudzu
Kukicha tea
Ladyfingers
Lamb's lettuce
Lavender blossoms
Leaf salads (bitter)
Leek
Lemon Balm (dried)
Lemon Balm (fresh)
Lemon peel
Lemongrass
Licorice root tea
Lily bulbs
Lime
Lime blossom tea
Linseed
Linseed (crushed)
Linseed oil
Liver smoothing tea
Loquate / Japanese medlar
Lotus roots
Lotus seeds
Lovage seeds
Luo Han Guo fruit

Lychee liqueur
Lye roll
Mango juice
Manioc flour
Mare's milk
Martini
Mascarpone cheese
Mayonnaise 50%
Mayonnaise 80%
Medlar
Mirabelle plum
Miso
Miso black (fermented)
Mixed Pickles
Morel, dried
Mu Erh Mushroom
Muesli
Mulberry fruit
Mulled Wine Spice
Multi-grain bread (gray bread)
Mung bean
Mung bean sprouting
Mussels
Mustard
Mustard Dijon
Mustard medium hot
Mustard sweet
Nasturtium (nose-twister or nose-tweaker)
Nectarine
Nettles
Noodles (wheat) with egg
Noodles (wheat, lasagne) with egg
Noodles (wheat, ribbon noodles) with egg
Noodles (wheat, spaghetti) with egg
Noodles (whole grain) with egg
Nori, purple seaweed, red algae
Octopus
Okra
Olive oil
Olives green
Onion (shallot)
Onion (spring onion)
Orange blossom
Orange dried peel
Orange grated peel
Orange jam
Orange peel
Oregano fresh
Oyster mushroom
Oyster shell powder
Palm oil
Parsley

Parsley root
Parsnip
Passion blossoms tea
Passion fruit
Peanut (roasted)
Peanut butter
Pear
Pearl barley
Pearl barley
Peas
Peas, green
Pepper powder (hot)
Peppermint
Peppermint tea
Pepperoni
Pepperoni, yellow, pitted, halved
Peppers
Peppers (sweet)
Peppers powder
Perch
Pickle
Pig blood
Pigeon
Pigeon egg
Plaice
Plum dried
Plums
Pork Bacon
Pork brain
Pork fat (lard)
Pork ham
Pork ham cooked
Pork ham smoked
Pork kidneys
Pork Lard
Pork lung
Pork marrow bones
Pork meat
Pork sausage (Bratwurst)
Pork/beef sausage (smoked)
Pork's intestine
Potato (mealy)
Potato flour
Prickly pear
Processed cheese 12%
processed cheese 30%
Prosecco
Psyllium seed
Pudding powder vanilla
Puff pastry
Pumpernickel (dark bread)
Pumpkin seed oil
Pumpkin seeds
Quail

Quail egg
Quince
Rabbit (wild)
Radicchio
Radish horseradish
Radish leaves
Raspberry
Raspberry jam
Raspberry leaf tea
Red beet
Red berry (without sugar)
Reishi mushroom
Ribworttea
Rice (Gaoliang / Sorghum)
Rice long grain rice
Rice mash
Rice noodles
Rice round grain
Rice starch
Rice sticky
Rice wild (nature rice)
Rose blossom tea
Rose hip
Rose leaf tea
Rucola
Rum
Rusk
Rye wholemeal bread
Safflower (Dyer's thistle / Hong Hua)
Salt
Salt (herbal)
Savory
Savoy cabbage / kale
Sea buckthorn
Sea cucumber
Sesame oil roasted
Sesame paste (Tahini)
Sesame, black
Shark
Sheep's milk yoghurt
Sherry (whine)
Shiitake, dried
Shrimps
Skim milk powder
Slug
Sourdough
Soy noodles
Soy Tofu smoked
Soybeans, black
Soybeans, blacks, fermented
Spelled (Dark) bread
Spelled flakes
Spelled grain
Spelled semolina

Spelled wholemeal flour
Spinach
Spurdog (spiny dogfish, Schillerlocken)
St. Benedict's thistle, blessed thistle, holy thistle, spotted thistle
Stevia (candyleaf, sweetleaf)
Strawberries
Strawberry jam
Strawberry Juice
Sugar - icing sugar
Sugar palm sugar
Sugar substitute (sweetener)
Sunflower seeds
Supplementary nutrition
Tabasco
Tea mixture uric acid lowering
Thyme dried
Toast bread (whole grain)
Tomato
Tomato dried
Tomato juice
Tomato paste
Tomato puree
Tonic Water
Trout
Trout (smoked)
Truffle
Tsampa (roasted barley flour)
Turkey breast meat
Turkey ham
Turmeric (yellow root)
Turnip
Turnips
Umeboshi paste
Valerian
Vanilla pod
Vanilla sugar natural
Vinegar Aceto Balsamico white
Wakame

Walnuts
Walnuts roasted
Watermelon
Wax gourd
Wheat
Wheat bran
Wheat bulgur
Wheat flakes
Wheat flatbread/pita bread
Wheat flour
Wheat flour whole grain
Wheat semolina
Wheat semolina for children
Wheat/Rye/Gray-black bread with yeast
Wheatgrass juice
Wheatgrass powder
Whey
White bread (baguette)
White bread (pretzel sticks)
White bread (roll)
White bread (wheat bread)
White breadcrumbs
White cabbage
White dumpling bread (wheat bread cut into chunks)
Whitefish
Whole grain bread
Wholemeal flour
Wild garlic (garlic spinach)
Wild herbs
Wild strawberries
Wormwood herb
Yam root, yam root tuber
Yarrow
Yeast
Yew nut
Yoghurt vanilla
Zucchini

10.2 Use ingredients: yes

Almond
Apple (sour)
Apple (sweet)
Arrowroot
Balm
Barley
Barley not peeled
Bean oil
Black-eyed peas
Blueberry juice
Broccoli
Buckwheat

Bulgur (cereals)
Butter organic
Carrot
Carrot (Early Carrot)
Carrot juice without sugar
Cashews
Cauliflower
Chamomile
Chickpeas
Chinese cabbage
Clementines
Coconut grated

Coix (seeds) YiYi Ren
Cooking oil
Coriander
Corn
Couscous
Cranberry
Cranberry juice
Créme fraiche cheese
Currant (black)
Currant (red)
Currant (white)
Elderberry blossom tee
Evening primrose oil
Fig
Fig dried
Ginger oil
Goose
Goose parts
Gooseberry
Gourd
Hawthorn
Hazelnuts
Kefir
Kidney beans (red)
Kohlrabi
Lentils
Lentils black
Lentils red
Lentils yellow
Lychee
Lychee in Preserved
Mallow (Malva sylvestris) blossom tea
Malt
Maple syrup
Margarine
Margarine (diet)
Millet
Millet flakes
Morel (black, dried)
Oat
Oat flakes (whole grain)
Oat flakes roasted
Oat flour
Oat fusion (baby food)
Oat milk
Octopus
Olives
Peanut oil
Peanuts
Pear juice
Pine nuts
Pinto beans speckled

Pistachios
Pork heart
Pork knuckle
Pork liver
Pork skin
Pork stomach
Potato
Quinoa
Rabbit liver
Rabbit meat
Radish
Radish black
Rapeseed oil
Raspberry dried (immature)
Red cabbage
Rice (fragrance)
Rice (whole grain)
Rice Basmati
Rice black
Rice flour
Rice red
Rice sweet
Rice variety any
Rye
Rye flour
Saffron
Sage
Salsify
Sauerkraut (cutted cabbage fermented)
Sesame oil
Sesame, white
Sorrel
Sour cherries
Soy flour
Soya Cuisine (soy cream)
Soybean milk
Soybeans
Soybeans, yellow
Sugar molasses
Sunflower oil
Sweet potato
Tangerine
Thistle oil
Topinambur
Vanilla
Vanilla powder
Vegetable juice
Walnut oil
Water
Water hot
Wheat germ oil

10.3 Use ingredients: little

Adzuki beans
Almond marzipan
Almond milk
Almond puree
Amaranth
Anchovy / Sardine
Anise (Common Fennel)
Apricot
Apricots
Aubergine
Bamboo shoots
Batavia
Beef bone marrow
Beef fillet
Beef heart
Beef liver
Beef lungs (calf)
Beef meat
Beef meat (calf)
Beef meatbones
Beef stomach
Black beans
Broad beans (thick beans)
Burdock root tea
Bush beans
Butter beans white
Calamari
Carambola (Star fruit)
Cherry juice
Chestnuts
Coconut flakes
Coconut milk
Cow's milk (1.5% fat)
Cow's milk (whole milk 3.5% fat)
Cumin (Caraway seed)
Dandelion (young plants)
Dandelionroots tea
Dates dried
Deer meat
Dill
Fennel tea
Fresh cheese
Grapefruit (Pomelo)
Grapefruit juice
Green spelt
Honey
Iceberg lettuce

Kiwi
Lamb's lettuce
Lettuce
Lima beans
Longane
Mackerel
Mango
Mold cheese
Mozzarella
Mullet
Oat meal
Onion white
Oysters
Papaya
Parmesan
Peaches
Peaches (canned)
Pheasant
Plum
Pomegranate
Pumpkin
Radish (white, green, purple-red)
Raisins
Rhubarb
Rice malt
Romaine lettuce / lettuce salad
Rose hip tea
Rosefish
Sago (cereals)
Salmon
Sour milk cheese 20%
Soybean oil
Sugar brown
Sugar candy white
Sugar cane sugar
Sugar fructose - fruit sugar
Sugar glucose - grapes sugar
Sugar Milk Sugar
Sugar white
Vinegar (Apple vinegar)
Vinegar (Red wine vinegar)
Vinegar Aceto Balsamico
White beans
Yarrow tea
Yogurt (natural, 1.5% fat)
Yogurt (natural, 3.5% fat)

10.4 Do not use contra-acting foods

Banana
Banana (cooking banana)
Beer (Pils)
Beer (Top-fermented German dark beer)
Black caraway
Black tea
Boxhorn clover seeds
Buttermilk
Cereal coffee
Chili (pod or ground)
Chives
Cinnamon ground
Cinnamon sticks
Clove
Cocoa
Cod
Coffee
Crab
Cream, sweet 30%
Curcuma
Curd cheese 20%
Curd cheese 40%
Curry
Curry paste red
Deer meat
Eel
Feta cheese
Garlic
Ginger fresh
Ginger powder
Goat
Goat and sheep's milk
Goat cheese
Goose egg
Green tea
Ground
Ground caraway
Hyssop
Juniper berry
Kumquats
Lamb bones
Lamb kidneys
Lamb liver
Lamb meat
Lamb shoulder
Lemon
Lemon juice

Lobster
Lovage
Marjoram
Mediterranean fish (cod, plaice, haddock, seaMineral water
Miso paste (soy bean paste)
Mustard seeds
Mutton
Mutton
Nutmeg
Onion read
Orange
Orange juice
Oregano dried
Pepper (ground)
Pepper Cayenne
Pepper white (ground)
Peppercorns
Pepperoni, red, pitted, halved
Peppers (rose peppers)
Pimento
Pineapple
Pineapple (from a can)
Pineapple juice without sugar
Poppy
Rabbit
Red wine
Rosemary
Sake
Seacrab
Sheep's milk
Shrimp
Sour cream 15% fat
Sour milk
Soy sauce
Soy Tofu
Spiny lobsters
Spirit
Star anise
Tarragon (Estragon)
Thyme
Tuna
Umeboshi plums (Japanese apricots)
Wheat beer
White wine
Wild boar meat
Wormwood
Yogi tea

11 Herbs and their effects

11.1 Basil

thermal effect: warm
taste: spicy, bitter
Dries out, leads down. Tonifies Yang and Qi, dissolves mucus-cold,
eliminates wind-cold.
It has a beneficial effect on flatulence and nausea, relaxing and soothing.
Good to fight emphysema, bronchitis, whooping cough, high blood
pressure, headache, mouth odor, warts, hiccup, gout, migraine.

11.2 Coriander

thermal effect: warm
taste: spicy
Driving sweat, reducing wind, draining moisture, tonifying and regulating
qi, eliminating wind-cold.
The essential oils are appetizing, digestive, cramping and soothing in
stomach and intestinal disorders.

11.3 Herbs various

Stimulates appetite. Effect different.
Appetizing, lots of trace elements and vitamins.

11.4 Cress

thermal effect: cool
taste: sweet
Moves and tonifies qi and blood, diuretic, cools in internal heat,
moisturizes lungs, triggers stagnation, heads upwards.
Diuretic, supports urination. Good to fight dry mouth, inner agitation, sore
throat, diabetes, kidney stones, gastrointestinal complaints, lung
problems, menstrual cramps or cancer.

11.5 Lily bulbs

thermal effect: cool
taste: sweet, bitter
Tonifies Yin, soothes Shen / Spirit. Moisturizes the lungs, clears heat and
stops coughing. Calms nerves, good to fight scaly skin. The onions and
the petals are added to ointments in the Orient, which can heal muscles
and tendons. White lily (astringent).

11.6 Parsley

thermal effect: warm
taste: bitter
Nourishes blood and liver, harmonizes liver and spleen, strengthens eyesight, preserves juices, contracts. Dissolves moisture and warms Yang.
Stimulates liver function, detoxifies. Forces urinating. Relieves flatulence.
Digestive and menstrual stimulating, birth-accelerating, memory-enhancing, blood-purifying, skin-smoothing.

11.7 Peppermint

thermal effect: cool
taste: spicy, bitter
Cools heat, expels mucus, dissipates wind-cold and wind-heat, moves stomach qi, releases congestion, tonifies, regulates and moves qi.
Relaxes, frees the lungs and the nose (inhale), regulates the cycle.
Stimulates bile flow and bile production, antispasmodic in gastrointestinal disorders, antimicrobial and antiviral.

11.8 Sage

thermal effect: neutral
taste: bitter, spicy
Expels slime, guides down, strengthens Qi, eliminates Wind-Heat, eliminate heat induced by Yin deficiency.
Good to fight yeast infections. The leaves have a digestive effect and are used in greasy foods. Antiperspirant effect. Helps to relieve coughing attacks. Dries out.

11.9 King Solomon's-seal

thermal effect: neutral
taste: sweet, bitter
Tonifies Yin and Qi, astringent, tonifies blood, eliminates wind-cold / heat-wetness.
Used to repair wounds or damaged tissue. Good to fight dry cough, earlier also tuberculosis and dysentery, as well as diarrhea and hemorrhoids.

11.10 Yam root, yam root tuber

thermal effect: neutral
taste: sweet
Tonifies Yin, Yang and Qi, reduces inner wind, dissolves wetness, warms Yang.
Solves cramps (in the gastrointestinal tract). Digestive through increased bile production. Anti-inflammatory in rheumatic diseases.
Mucolytic agent for coughing. Relief of menopausal symptoms.

12 Basics of Nutrition

The basic principles of nutrition described herein are general recommendations. They are not aimed at a specific form of therapy. Recommendations concerning a therapy have priority.

12.1 Nutrition

Regular meals in a relaxed atmosphere. A warm breakfast is considered a good start into the day.
The main meals ought to be taken for lunch – supper in the early evening. Pay attention to feeling hungry or sated: don't eat too much nor remain hungry is the rule
Prepare the meals freshly from natural, regional products. Frozen, heat-conserved, industrially prepared or foodstuffs cooked in the microwave oven are rejected.
Choice of foodstuffs according to the season: more cooling food in summer, more warming food in winter.
Eat cooked food at least twice a day. Food and drinks ought to be lukewarm, never ice-cold or hot.
Raw vegetables, briefly cooked vegetables, freshly squeezed juices and mineral water are not recommended. Milk and dairy products are only included in the diet if they don't cause problems. Don't use therapeutic recipes over a longer period without consulting your doctor or therapist.

Varied food
Enjoy the diversity of foodstuffs. Characteristics of a balanced nutrition are variety, suitable combination and a balanced quantity of rich and low energy foodstuffs (on one hand avoiding undersupply with essential nutrients and on the other hand to take to many undesirable substances).

A lot of Cereal Products - and Potatoes
Bread, pasta, rice, cereal flakes (best wholemeal) as well as potatoes contain almost no fat, but many vitamins, mineral nutrients, trace elements, roughage and secondary plant substances. These foodstuffs ought to be taken with low-fat side dishes.

Vegetables and Fruit – „Take Five" every day ... 5 portions of vegetables and fruit a day, as fresh as possible, briefly cooked, or maybe one portion as a juice – ideal as a side dish to every meal as well as snack between meals: Thus a lot of vitamins, mineral nutrients as well as roughage and secondary plant substances

Daily milk and dairy products
Milk and Dairy Products every Day, once or twice per Week Fish; meat, sausages as well as eggs moderately. These foodstuffs contain valuable nutrients like calcium in the milk, iodine selenium and omega-3 fat acids in saltwater fish. Meat is favorable due to its high content of disposable iron and the vitamins B1, B6 and B12. Quantities of 300 – 600 g meat and sausage per week are sufficient. Prefer low-fat products, especially in meat- and dairy products.

Low-fat and fatty Foodstuffs
Fat supplies us with essential fat acids and fatty foodstuffs contain also fat-soluble vitamins. Fat is high in energy; therefore much fat in the food may cause overweight, possibly also cancer. Too many saturated fat acids may further a tendency for cardio-vascular diseases in the long term. Prefer vegetable oils and fats (e.g. rapeseed-, olive-, soya-oils and solid fats produced therefrom). Beware of invisible fat in meat- and dairy products, pastry and sweets as well as in fast-food and convenience foods. 70 – 90 g fat per day is sufficient.

Moderately Sugar and Salt
Take sugar and foods/drinks containing various kinds of sugar (e.g. glucose syrup) only occasionally. Use herbs and spices as well as a little salt creatively. Prefer salt containing iodine.

Plenty of Liquids
Water is absolutely essential. Drink 1-2 l liquids every day. Prefer water (with or without gas) and other low-calorie drinks. Alcoholic drinks should not be taken.

Tasty Dishes, carefully cooked
Cook the meals with as low temperatures and as short as possible, using little water and fat – this preserves the original taste, keeps the nutrients intact and prevents the production of harmful compounds.

Take time and enjoy the food
Take your Time and enjoy your Food
Eating consciously helps to eat right. The eye enjoys food, too. It's fun, invites to enjoy varied dishes and stimulates the feeling of satiety.

Watch your Weight and stay in Motion
A balanced diet and a lot of exercise and sport (30 – 60 min/day) are a healthy combination. The right weight furthers well-being and health. Thermals, directional effectiveness, digestive power

There are various criteria for judging the effectiveness of herbs and foodstuffs.

The use of certain herbs and ingredients is based on observations of the effects on the body which these foodstuffs, herbs and spices show after having eaten them. The medical science has developed following system: Every ingredient or herb has a directional effectiveness. Furthermore, there are herbs which have a special effect on certain organs.

The basic condition for a healthy metabolism is to obtain sufficient energy from food and that the digestive process doesn't use too much energy. An easily digestible meal makes content and sated, doesn't cause flatulence and fatigue after the meal. The perfect spices increase the healthiness of our meals. Very often, just small doses of herbs and spices will suffice. They are not used to make us sated, but to help our digestive organs to digest the food.

12.2 Recipes

The recipes list the ingredients to be used and the cooking instructions show how the dish is prepared. The list of ingredients shows the concerned quantities as well as the relevance for the therapy. If you find „less than mentioned", try to comply or find an alternative from the „list of recommended foodstuffs". Mostly it shall result just in a small change of taste when you simply avoid this ingredient.

Mild cooking methods: boiling, stewing, poaching, steaming
Strong cooking methods: barbecuing, roasting, frying, smoking
Balanced cooking methods: deep-frying, baking brick
Deep-freezing and warming in the microwave oven should be avoided (denaturalization).

12.3 Foodstuffs

Foodstuffs have an effect on body and soul like medicinal herbs, only a very much milder one. Dietary advice is mainly based on regional foodstuffs. The knowledge about the effects of each foodstuff and the knowledge, when which foodstuff shall be used, is based on the orthodox school of medicine. Use ecologic-organic products, if possible. As everything should be cooked for a long time due to a better digestability and very rarely eaten raw, the food agrees with everyone.

The classification of the foodstuffs according to their effect on the body is the basis in order to achieve a harmonious status of health.

Dietary advisors do not recommend certain foodstuffs for everyone. The individual diet is tailor-made for the individual constitution.

Buy only fresh and ripe fruit and vegetables. You ought to leave unripe fruit and vegetables and such with brown spots and wilted leaves behind in the market. In this case take deep-frozen goods (never ready-to-serve dishes!). Fruit and vegetables are deep-frozen immediately after harvesting and often contain more vitamins and minerals than the goods from the vegetable shelf. Whereas conserved or tinned goods contain very much less biological substances. Also, salt, sugar and others are mostly added to the latter. Never leave the foodstuffs in the water after washing them to avoid that many vital substances get drowned. Clean salads, fruit and vegetables immediately before serving.

Please make sure of the hygienic processing of foodstuffs. Clean your salads, fruit and vegetables carefully. When cooking with meat, prepare all ingredients first and then process the meat products. Clean the worktop and tools very carefully. Wooden surfaces ought to be treated with a mild disinfectant regularly in order to reduce germination.
Store fruit and vegetables separately, if possible. Harvested fruit and vegetables are still alive and emit e.g. ethylene gas, which makes other products ripen and age faster. Keep meat and fish in the closed packaging or store them in the fridge in closed containers.

12.4 Herbs

There are some basic rules for storing medicinal herbs. On principle, herbs must be protected from direct sunlight, humidity and heat.

Containers for the storage of herbs may be glasses, ceramic jars and even plastic containers. However, plastic is a rather unsuitable material and should only be a short-term solution. In case of glass containers, use a dark material.

Medicinal herbs cannot be kept for any long period. The shelf life of herbs is limited. However, it can be prolonged with suitable storage. The place should be dark, rather cool and absolutely dry. A wooden medicine cabinet, placed not directly next to a source of heat, would be ideal. Never buy large quantities of herbs so as not to have to throw them away. Label the container with the name of the herb and the date of harvesting or processing.

13 Other dietic-books

The following syndromes of dietetics, TCM or for a therapy supplement for cancer are available.

Dietetics
E001. Nutrition of the infant - baby food
E002. Nutrition during lactation
E003. Nutrition in old age
E004. Nutrition of children and adolescents
E005. Nutrition of athletes
E006. Light weight
E007. Pregnancy
E008. Full food

Protein and electrolyte - kidneys
E009. (hemodialysis) dialysis treatment
E010. Acute renal failure
E011. Chronic renal insufficiency
E012. Nephrotic syndrome
E013. Kidney stones (nephrolithiasis)

Gastrointestinal tract - pancreas
E014. Acute pancreatitis (inflammation of the pancreas)
E015. Chronic pancreatitis (inflammation of the pancreas)

Gastrointestinal tract - small intestine and large intestine
E016. Acute obstipation (constipation)
E017. Chronic obstipation (constipation)
E018. Colon irritabile
E019. Diverticulitis
E020. Acquired lactose intolerance (lactose malabsorption)
E021. Fructose malabsorption
E022. Glutensensitive enteropathy (celiac disease)
E023. Colectomy
E024. Short Bowel Syndrome

Gastrointestinal tract - liver, gallbladder, bile ducts
E025. Acute and chronic hepatitis (inflammation of the liver)
E026. Cholelithiasis (bile stones)
E027. fatty liver
E028. cirrhosis

Gastrointestinal tract - Stomach and duodenal intestine
E029. Acute gastritis
E030. Chronic gastritis
E031. Stomach bleeding
E032. Ulcus ventriculi and duodenal ulcer
E033. Condition after gastric surgery

Gastrointestinal tract - oral cavity and esophagus
E034. Stomatitis
E035. Esophageal carcinoma (esophageal cancer)
E036. Refluosophagitis (heartburn)

Special diseases
E037. Phenylketonuria (PKU)
E038. Rheumatic joint diseases

Metabolism
E039. Obesity (overweight)
E040. Diabetes mellitus
E041. Eating disorders (underweight)

Fat metabolism
E042. Hypercholesterolaemia (increased cholesterol level)
E043. Hepatic Encephalopathy

Heart and circulation
E044. Arteriosclerosis (arterial calcification)
E045. Heart insufficiency
E046. Hypertension
E047. Hyperuricaemia and gout

Changed nutrient requirements
E048. In case of fever
E049. For malignant diseases
E050. After burns
E051. Radiation and chemotherapy

CANCER
E100. Pancreatic cancer
E101. Bladder cancer
E102. Blood cancer (leukemia)
E103. Breast cancer
E104. Colorectal cancer
E105. Gastric cancer
E106. Kidney cancer
E107. Esophageal cancer

TCM
E200. Bladder - moisture heat in the bladder
E201. Bladder - moisture and cold in the bladder
E202. Bladder - emptiness and cold in the bladder
E203. Large intestine - external cold affects the large intestine
E204. Large intestine - moisture heat in the large intestine
E205. Large intestine - heat blocks the intestine II acute
E206. Large intestine - dryness of the colon
E207. Large intestine - Yang deficiency (cold)
E208. Heart - Blood insufficiency
E209. Heart - Blood stagnation
E210. Heart - Fire
E211. Heart - Hot mucus clogs the heart pores

E212. Heart - Cold mucus clogs the heart pores
E213. Heart - Qi deficiency
E214. Heart - Yang deficiency
E215. Heart - Yin deficiency
E216. Liver - Ascending Liver Yang
E217. Liver - Blood deficiency
E218. Liver - Blood stagnation
E219. Liver - Moisture heat in liver and gall bladder
E220. Liver - Fire
E221. Liver - Gall bladder Qi-Empty
E222. Liver - Cold in the liver meridian
E223. Liver - Qi stagnation
E224. Liver - Wind
E225. Liver - Wind with ascending liver Yang
E226. Liver - Wind with blood anemic
E227. Liver - Wind with extreme heat
E228. Lung - Qi deficiency
E229. Lung - Mucus-moisture in the lungs
E230. Lung - Mucus-heat in the lungs
E231. Lung - Mucus-cold in the lungs
E232. Lung - Dryness of the lungs
E233. Lung - Wind-heat attacks the lungs
E234. Lung - Wind-cold affects the lungs
E235. Lung - Yin deficiency
E236. Stomach - Bloodstagnation
E237. Stomach - Fire
E238. Stomach - Cold with liquid
E239. Stomach - Nutrition stagnation
E240. Stomach - Qi deficiency
E241. Stomach - Rebellious Qi
E242. Stomach - Yin Emptiness
E243. Spleen - Heat and moisture attack the spleen
E244. Spleen - Coldness and moisture affects the spleen
E245. Spleen - Qi deficiency
E246. Spleen - Qi deficiency + Declining spleen Qi
E247. Spleen - Qi deficiency + spleen does not control the blood
E248. Spleen - Yang deficiency
E249. Kidney - Heart and kidney no longer communicate
E250. Kidney - Jing deficiency
E251. Kidney - Kidneys cannot receive the Qi
E252. Kidney - Qi is not stable
E253. Kidney - Yang deficiency
E254. Kidney - Yin deficiency

For further information visit di-book.com.